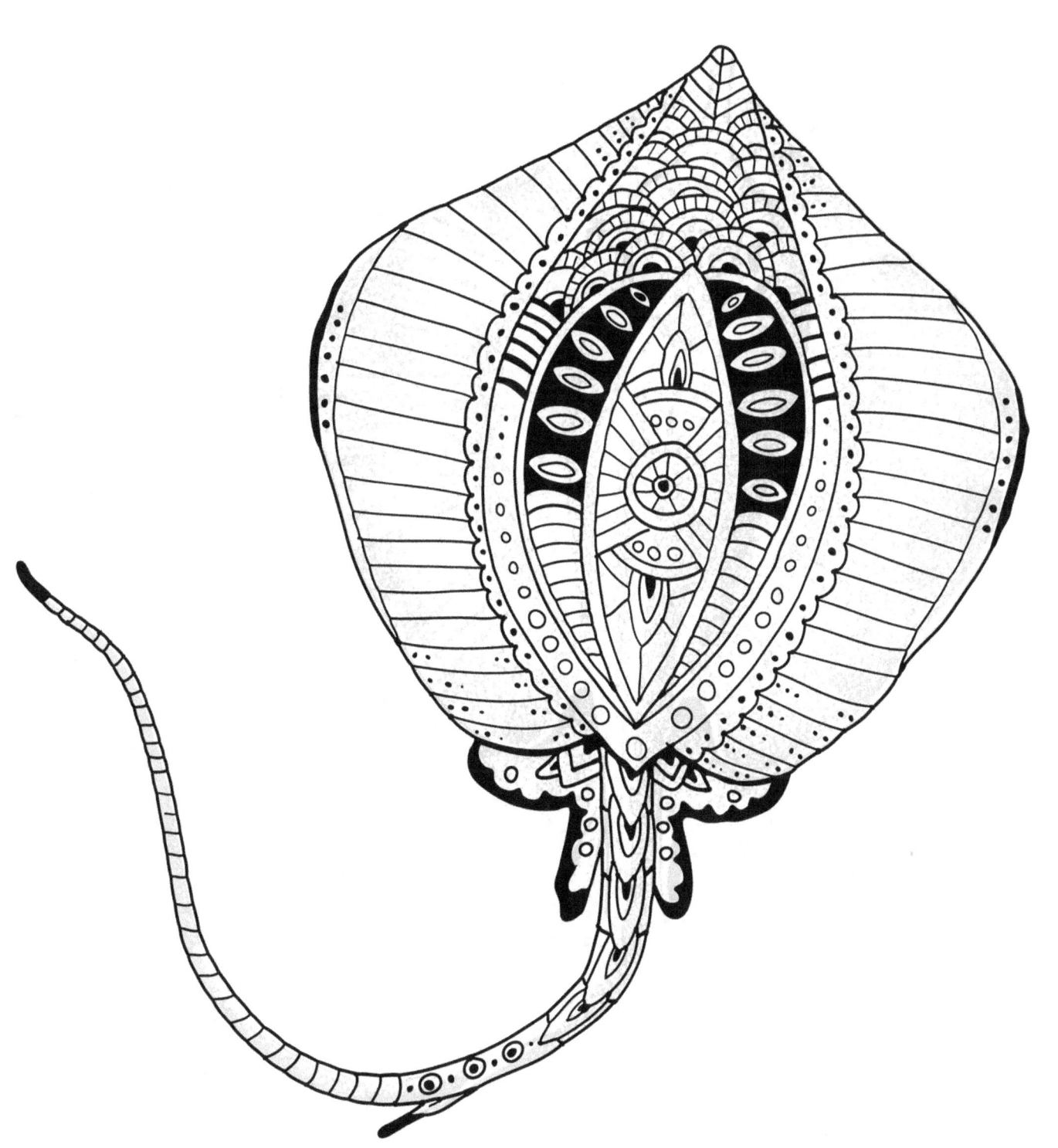

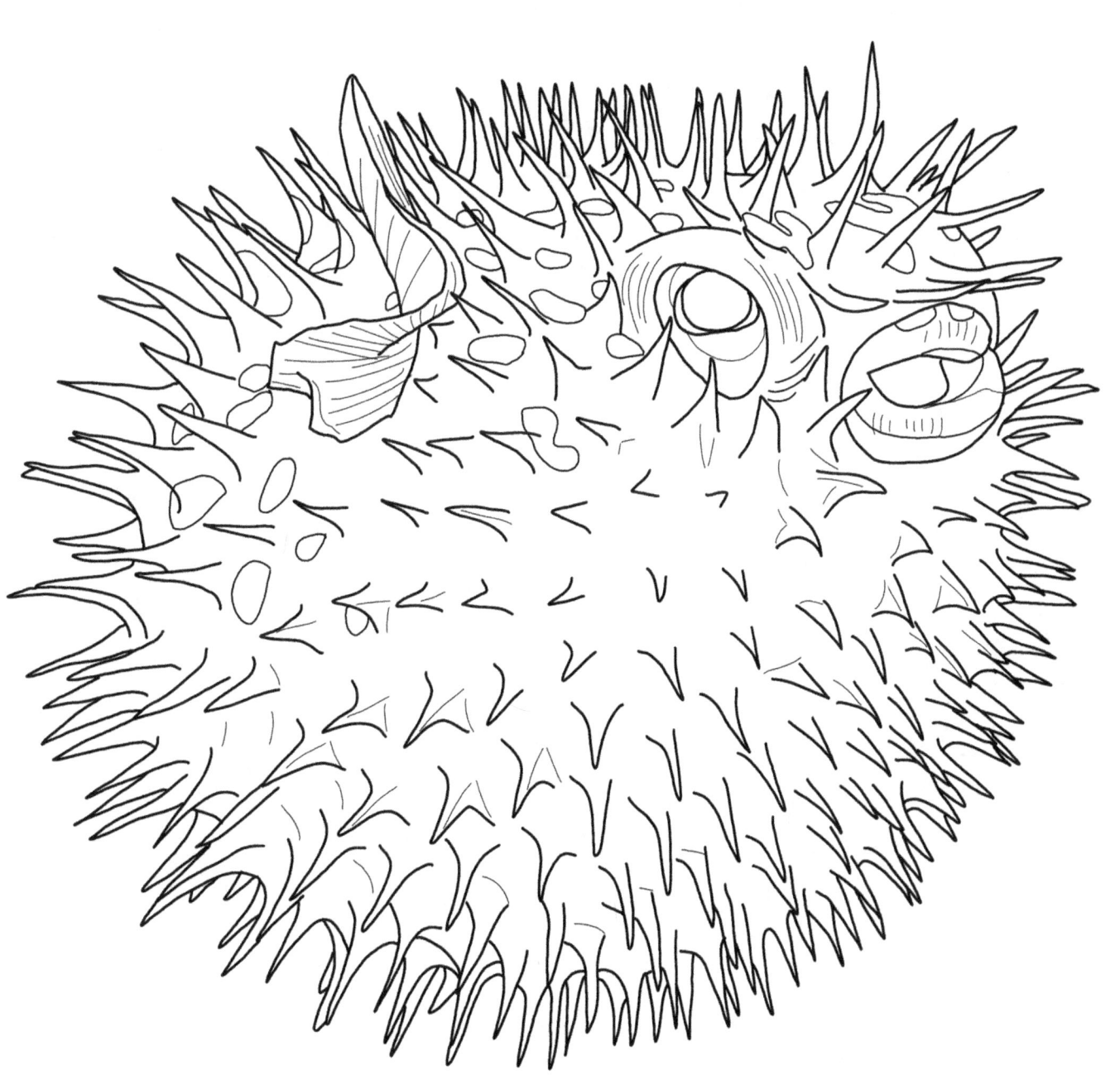

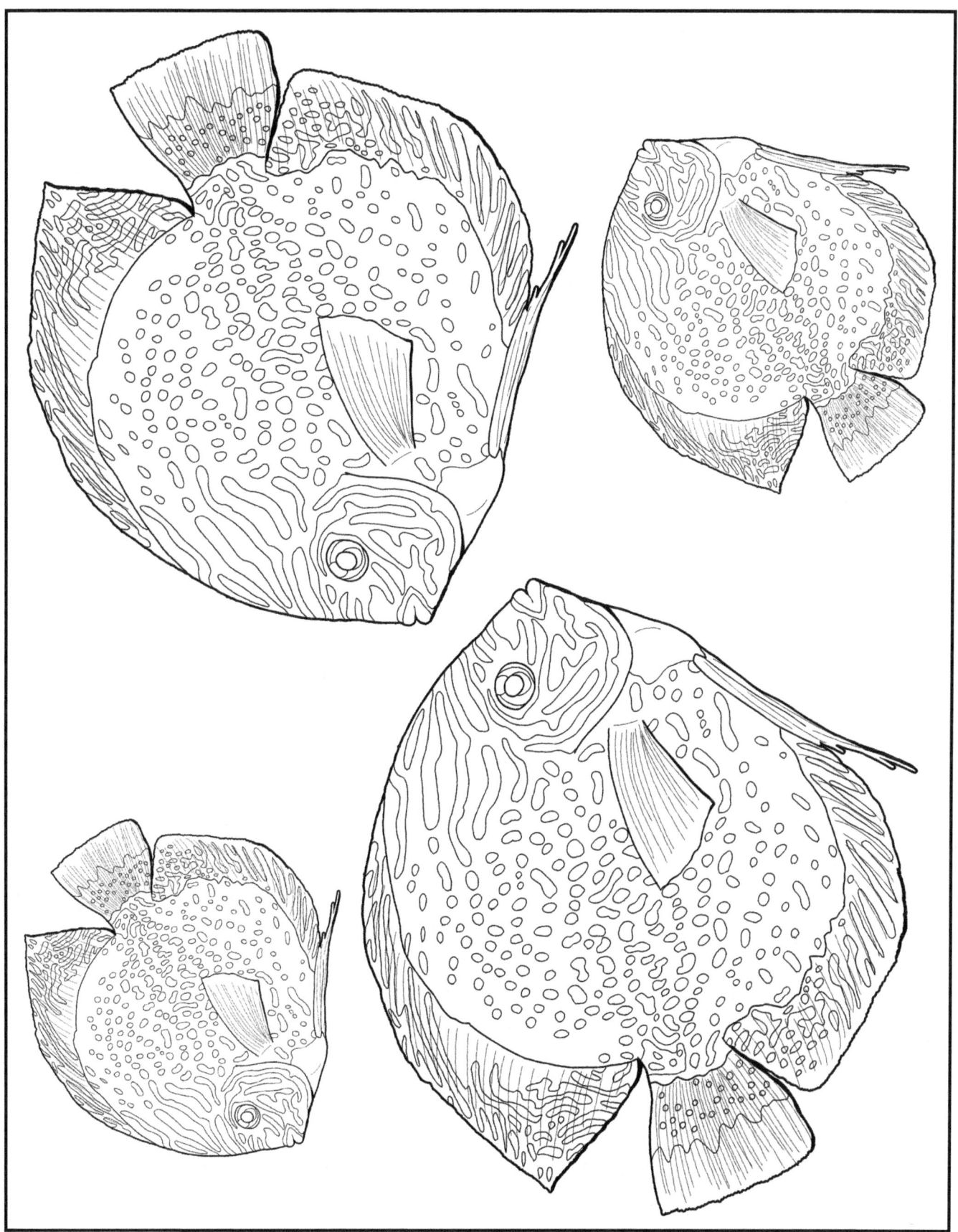

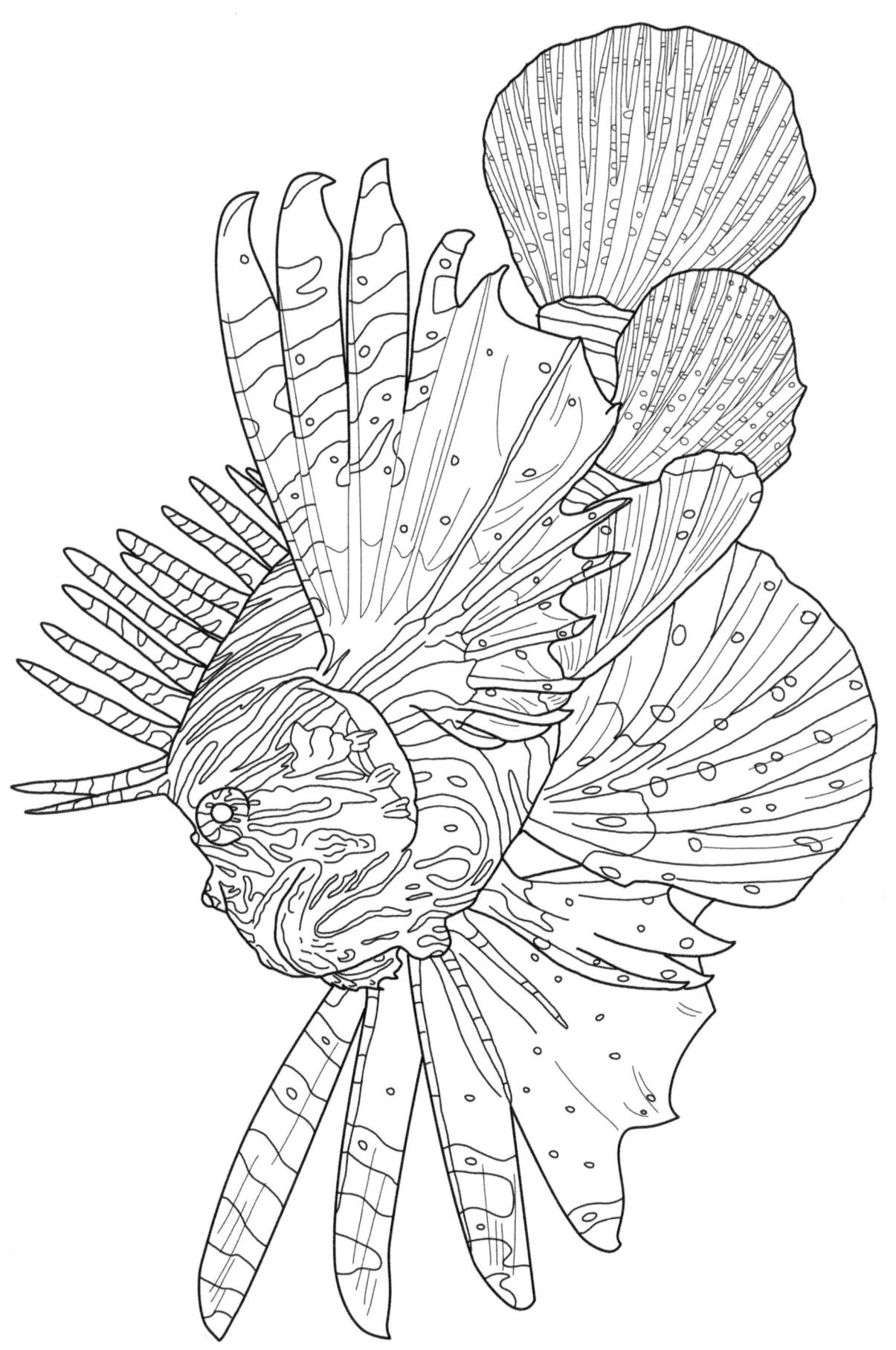

STARFISH & SEASHELLS

KOI FISH

STINGRAY

SEAHORSE

BLUE DRAGON NUDIBRANCH

CUTTLEFISH

JELLYFISH

ORCA - KILLER WHALE

BETTA FISH

EMPEROR PENGUINS

LEAFY SEA DRAGON

CORAL MANDALA

GOLDFISH

PUFFER FISH

SEA TURTLE

PELICAN

SCALAR (ANGEL) FISH

MANATEE

TROPICAL FISH

LEOPARD MORAY EEL

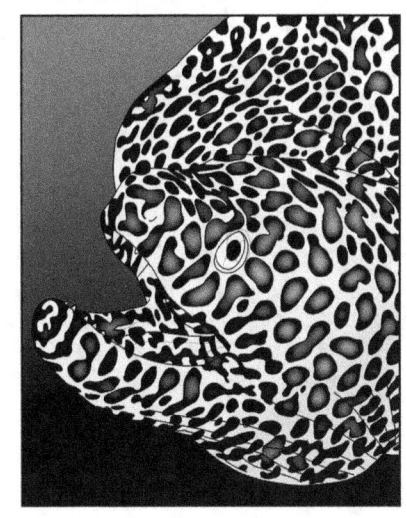

TIGER SHARK

MOON CRAB

COCONUT OCTOPUS

DOLPHINS

TROPICAL FISH

DISCUS

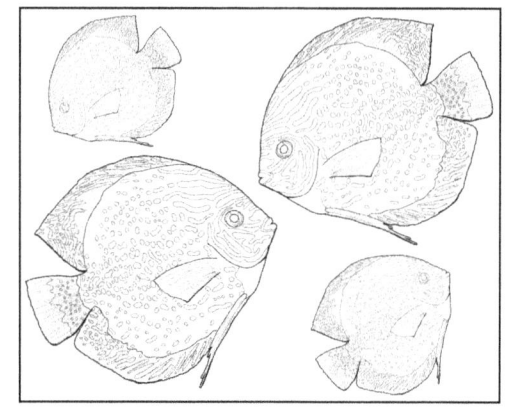

WALRUS

MARLIN

CLOWN FISH

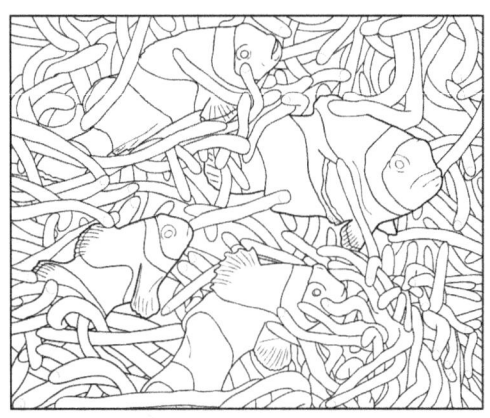

LIONFISH

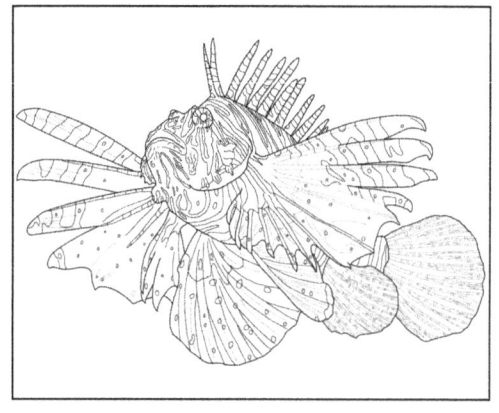

COLOR TEST SQUARES

TEST YOUR COLORS HERE AND USE THIS
PAGE AS A REFERENCE GUIDE

www.ingramcontent.com/pod-product-compliance
Lightning Source LLC
Chambersburg PA
CBHW081415280526
45788CB00009B/3109